GREG ELVIS

OMAN TRAVEL GUIDE 2024

Discover Oman: Your Essential Travel Guide to Arabian Wonders, Cultural Riches, and Natural Beauty in the Heart of the Middle East

Contents

1

Introduction

Welcome to Oman, the land of sun, sand and smiles! Imagine a place where camels leap over golden sand dunes, turquoise waters sparkle like jewels, and ancient walls whisper history.

Feel the weight of time at Nizwa Fort, Its huge walls tell the story of the battle. Explore ancient Bahla, where adobe houses tell stories from another era. Walk through the ruins of Al Barleed, once a bustling port but now a place where silent giants guard the secrets of the sea.

Snorkel among colorful fish in the fjords of Musandam, nicknamed the Arabia's Norway for its dramatic cliffs and emerald waterways. Kayak through Wadi Shab, past towering rocks and the sun's rays hitting the water. Or enjoy the waves while windsurfing in Salalah and enjoy the scent of incense carried by the wind.

It's the whisper of a warm desert wind, the caress of turquoise waves, and the warmth of thousands of friendly smiles. Here, history whispers between the stones, adventure lurks around every corner, and peace washes in like the tides of the ocean.

A Brief History of Oman

Oman's history is woven into a tapestry of ancient civilizations that flourished along its rugged coastline. Archaeological excavations indicate the existence of an early settlement in the 3rd millennium BCE. A historic port, the city of Sohar has grown into a thriving trading center connecting Oman with Mesopotamia and ancient civilizations.

Oman's maritime heritage reached its climax during the period of the Omani Empire (17th to 19th centuries). Omani sailors and seafarers skilled in seafaring crossed the Indian Ocean and established trade routes from East Africa to the Indian subcontinent. The Omani Navy ruled the seas with its distinctive wooden dhows, making Oman a formidable naval power.

Oman is considered a unique hotbed of Ibadi Islam, a moderate and tolerant form of faith. Ibadi doctrine emphasizes the coexistence of religions, a philosophy that has shaped Oman's cultural landscape. The country's religious tolerance fosters a harmonious society where different religious beliefs are respected, creating a special atmosphere of unity.

The rise of the Al Bu Said dynasty in the 18th century marked the beginning of a new era for Oman. Under the visionary leadership of Sultan Qaboos bin Said, Oman underwent remarkable transformation. The Sultan's rule modernized infrastructure, education, and healthcare, and brought Oman into the 21st century while preserving its rich cultural heritage.

As you explore Oman's interior, you will discover that the ancient city of Nizwa is a living testament to the country's historical importance. A symbol of Oman's strength, the imposing Nizwa Fort dates back to his 17th century. The bustling Nizwa Souq, with its maze of alleyways, reflects the centuries-old tradition of trade and commerce that has flourished in the heart of Oman.

In the southern Dhofar region, ancient frankincense trade routes tell stories of wealth and cultural exchange. The city of Salalah, with its lush landscape during the monsoon season, was an important port along these trade routes.

The Land of Frankincense, a UNESCO World Heritage Site, preserves the archaeological remains of this historic trade. Oman's architectural heritage is a testament to its rich history. Magnificent fortresses and castles such as Nahal Citadel and Jabrin Castle are considered impressive guardians of the past.

2

Planning Your Journey to Oman

Best Times to Visit

Choosing when to visit will be an important decision in order to reveal the wonders of this country in all its glory. This is the key to uncovering each chapter of Oman's history, a perfect combination of climate, culture and captivating experiences.

October to November

As the passion of Oman's summer fades, autumn brings with it a quiet charm. From October to November, Oman's landscape takes on a golden hue and temperatures range from a comfortable 25 to 35 degrees Celsius (77 to 95 degrees Fahrenheit).

This time of year is a great time to escape the summer heat and explore ancient forts, stroll through fragrant souks, and enjoy the splendor of the coast as you enjoy the breeze.

December to February

Winter in Oman is a serenade of mild days and clear nights. Temperatures in the Sultanate from December to February range from 15 to 25 degrees Celsius. Muscat becomes a paradise where you can enjoy outdoor activities against the backdrop of clear skies.

It's the ideal time to explore the intricate Grand Mosque, stroll through the Royal Gardens, or explore the enchanting desert while enjoying the gentle winter weather.

March-April

March-April marks the awakening of nature in Oman, painting the landscape with a riot of colour. With temperatures in the 20s and 30s, spring is the perfect time for a variety of explorations.

Experience the underground wonders of Al Fouta Caves or hike through the flowering orchards of Jebel Akhdar. Each experience unfolds against the vibrant canvas of Oman in spring.

May to September

Warm temperatures of 30 to 45 degrees Celsius (86 to 113 degrees Fahrenheit) during the summer months lend a unique magic to Oman's landscapes. The coastal areas, especially Salalah during the kharif season, turns into a green paradise. Lush greenery and mild temperatures provide a refreshing escape from the summer heat, making it an alternative summer destination in the Sultanate.

Calendar of Festivals and Celebrations

Plan your visit with Oman's vibrant cultural calendar. Muscat Festival in January, Salalah Tourism Festival during Khareef, and Nizwa Date Festival in October are just a few of the events that offer deeper insight into Oman's rich heritage and add even more cultural richness to your trip .

When choosing the best time to travel to Oman, it's not just the weather that matters. Our mission is to create experiences that touch the soul of every season. Whether you seek the bright colors of spring, the tranquility of winter, or the unique charm of Khareef, Oman invites you to discover its wonders in a time that suits your desire for a truly enriching adventure.

Visa Requirements to Oman

Whether you're drawn to the mystique of the Empty Quarter desert, the architectural wonders of Nizwa or the turquoise charm of Musandam Fjords, Oman promises an unforgettable adventure.

However, before your Oman journey begins, we first clarify the visa and entry requirements to ensure a smooth and stress-free trip.

Visa Free

For 103 lucky nationalities, including nationals of the United States, Canada, and most European countries, Oman offers a warm welcome with visa-free entry for up to 14 days.

That means all you have to do is hop on a plane, land in Muscat and explore the wonders of this fascinating country. Remember to bring a valid passport with at least 6 months validity and get ready to fall in love with the magic of Oman.

Electronic Visa

Don't worry if your passport doesn't qualify for visa-free protection. Oman's e-visa system is simple. Simply visit the Royal Oman Police e-visa portal, fill out the application form, upload your documents (passport, photo, flight ticket) and pay the visa fee.

Your e-visa will arrive in your inbox within a few days. Print it now and keep it in your travel bag.

What Documents Do You Need?

Here's what you'll need to have in order for your e-Visa application to sail through smoothly:

- A valid passport with at least six months' remaining validity.
- A recent digital photograph.
- Proof of confirmed accommodation booking in Oman.
- Proof of return flight or onward travel.
- A credit or debit card that is currently valid to pay the visa charge.

Landing in Oman

Once you land in Oman, prepare for easy immigration formalities. Please have your passport, e-visa (if applicable), and arrival documents ready for inspection. The immigration officer may also ask you about the purpose of your visit and how long you plan to stay.

Remember that politeness plays a big role. Our friendly smiles and courteous manners will ensure a smooth entrance. Beyond formalities: Once you understand the visa and entry requirements, get a feel for the spirit of Oman.

Here are some additional tips for a comfortable stay.

Please respect local customs and dress modestly. Oman is a Muslim country, so covering your shoulders and knees is recommended, especially when visiting religious sites.

Learn some basic Arabic phrases. A simple "Shukran" (thank you) or "Marhaba" (hello) goes a long way in showing respect and appreciation.

Haggling is part of the fun of souks (markets). Don't be afraid to negotiate good-naturedly for souvenirs and spices.

Stay hydrated, Oman's desert climate can be hot and sunny, so it's important to stay hydrated. Please disconnect to reconnect.

Oman is a place to relax and enjoy the moment. Put down your phone and immerse yourself in the beautiful scenery and the warmth of the Omani people.

With these tips and a valid visa (or the freedom to enter visa-free), you'll be ready for an unforgettable Oman adventure. Pack your bags, shake off your surprise, and let yourself be enchanted by the charm of this Arabian gem. Oman is waiting for you!

How to Get to Oman

Before setting off on your Oman journey, let's take a look at how to get to this fascinating country.

For those who crave the freedom of flying, Oman's international airports, Muscat International Airport (MCT) and Salalah Airport (SLL), welcome you with open arms (and runways).MAs you descend, the rugged peaks of the Hajar Mountains greet you, promising adventures to come.

Airlines such as Emirates, Qatar Airways and Oman Air have created connectivity networks from around the world, making Oman an accessible playground for those with wanderlust. Whether you're traveling from bustling Dubai or quiet Singapore, your trip itself will be a taste of Oman's festivals.

For those seeking a more romantic approach, Oman is full of maritime charm. Cruise ships such as MSC Fantasia and Costa Diadema sail the turquoise waters of the Arabian Sea, offering glimpses of rugged coastlines and charming fishing villages.

As you approach Muscat, the Sultan Qaboos Grand Mosque, a masterpiece of Islamic architecture, emerges from the mist, its golden minaret soaring into the sky. A vibrant harbor with the scent of spices and a cacophony of seagulls, ready to take you on an Omani adventure.

Oman's road system winds through the mountains and along the coast, like a ribbon waiting to be unfolded. Start your adventure by renting a car in Dubai or Muscat. Stop at a roadside souk (market) to get a taste of local life, haggle over intricately woven rugs, and refuel with Oman's sunny dates.

The streets of Oman are the canvas and the journey itself is the destination. No matter how you arrive, Oman promises an unforgettable stay.

Getting Around Oman

Oman has very little public transportation. It's easy to travel between major cities by bus, but to really see all of the country, you can sign up for a tour, hire a guide, or jump on the back of a bus and ride your own bike on your own. You need to use transportation.

By Car

The easiest way to get around the country is to drive yourself. An ever-expanding modern road network now covers most parts of the country, and driving is mostly easy, although it's not without some challenges.

Driving standards leave much to be desired, and the country's road accident and death toll is depressingly high (although not as high as in neighboring UAE). Always drive defensively, expect the unexpected, and be prepared for a madman in a Land Cruiser to hurtle at you at 150km/h. Traffic in Oman is on the right.

Typical speed limits are 120 km/h on dual carriageways, 100 km/h on single carriageways, and 60 km/h or 80 km/h in built-up areas. The car is equipped with a speed warning system that beeps (irritatingly) when it reaches 120km/h. Some major highways are monitored by speed cameras.

The most common road hazards include vehicles driving without lights on at night. A vehicle suddenly passes in front of you at high speed without blinking. Livestock roaming the roads, especially goats and (especially in Salalah) camels.

These cars can be seen in towns and villages across the country, but in many places the paint is peeling and there are no warning signs. If you run into one at 80 miles per hour, you'll be in for a nasty surprise.

For example, running a red light is punishable by two days in jail. Seat belts are also required and failure to wear a seat belt will result in an on-the-spot $10 fine. Oman is also known for its laws that require drivers to keep their cars clean.

Car Rental

Car rental is relatively cheap. International car rental companies offer cars for around 13-15 OR per day, which can be around 35 OR for a 4WD vehicle. Local companies may be able to provide you with vehicles for as little as 10 OR, but of course these vehicles may not be in as good a condition as those you rent from more reputable companies.

Please note that most car rental companies do not rent vehicles to anyone under 21 years of age. Petrol is very cheap by European standards, around 20p per litre.

By Bus and Minibus

All major cities in the country are connected by buses. In an emergency, it is enough to travel between large cities in the country, but no more.

Buses are mainly operated by the state-owned Oman National Transport Company (ONTC; www.ontcoman.com), but this site is not yet operational at the time of writing, and there are several buses on the Muscat-Salalah route. Private transportation companies also operate.

The bus is fairly fast and comfortable, but there are only 2-3 departures a day and it can be difficult to get information about exactly where and when it departs (although buses often If you use ONTC Concrete, you'll be able to learn about its distinctive baths).

Within large cities (particularly Muscat), taxis and minibuses (also known as "baisa buses") provide local transportation. It's basically a white and orange minivan that can carry up to 15 passengers in a small space.

These are used primarily by low-wage expatriates from the Indian subcontinent and are by far the cheapest form of transportation, but finding where the micro bases are can be difficult.

The vehicles are not marked, so you just have to ask around (or wave at everything you pass) until you find the vehicle that will take you where you want to go.Outside of Muscat, drivers are unlikely to speak more than a few words of English.

By Taxi

In large cities, taxis are the easiest way to get around. These are easy to spot thanks to their white and orange paint job, and are usually fairly easy to spot with just a sign posted on the side of the road. All taxis in Oman are not metered, so you'll need to agree on a price and negotiate hard before getting in.

While locals expect to spend no more than 1-2 OR on most intra-city trips (up to around 5 OR for long-distance trips within Muscat), foreigners can expect to spend significantly more than their quota.

You are likely to pay up to 20% more than you expected, and in some situations it can be up to twice as much. These prices depend on your bargaining power.

In Muscat, virtually everyone speaks at least a basic level of English. Outside of Muscat, only speak Arabic. Taxi can also operate as a shared taxi where 3 or her 4 passengers share the fare.MShared taxis operate both within cities and on long distance routes between cities and are a convenient alternative to buses.

However, this system works on an ad-hoc basics, requiring you to shop around locally to find the best place to pick up a shared taxi, which may prove more of a hassle than it's worth.

Packing Essentials to Oman

Mastering the art of packing is important to make your expedition go smoothly and have unforgettable moments.

Here are some insightful packing tips specific to your Oman adventure:

Remember modesty and dress light

Oman's climate is scorching from deserts to cool mountainous regions. Pack it with light, breathable fabric to combat the heat. However, remember that the local culture values modesty. Long, loose clothing is not only polite, but also protects you from the sun.

Sturdy shoes

Whether you're hiking the dramatic wadis or navigating the golden dunes of the Wahiba Dunes, comfortable, durable shoes are a must. Choose closed-toe shoes to protect your feet from hot sand and rocks.

Sunscreen Basics

The sun in Oman is intense, especially at its peak. To protect yourself from the strong sun, bring a wide-brimmed hat, sunglasses with UV protection, and sunscreen with a high SPF. Carry a reusable water bottle with you to remember to stay hydrated.

A practical daypack

A small and durable daypack that will be your faithful companion as you explore Oman's treasures. Perfect for carrying essentials such as water, snacks, maps, camera, and souvenirs bought along the way.

Cultural considerations

Respect for Omani customs is of the utmost importance. Include a scarf or shawl when packing so a woman can cover her shoulders and hair when visiting religious sites. It can get cool at night, especially in mountainous areas, so we recommend bringing a light jacket or sweater.

Camera

Capture the essence of your adventures by packing your reliable camera or smartphone and plenty of storage space. With a mobile battery, you will never miss a beautiful moment. An international adapter is essential to charge your device.

First Aid Kit

A simple first aid kit is essential for every traveller. Add bandages, disinfectant wipes, painkillers, and any necessary personal medications. It is important to always be prepared for minor emergencies.

Insect Repellent

Certain areas of Oman are prone to insects, so carrying a good quality insect repellent is a wise choice. This allows you to enjoy the breathtaking scenery without being distracted by annoying bites.

Cash and Cards

Credit cards may be accepted in larger cities and tourist areas, but it's a good idea to carry some cash, especially if you're going to remote areas or local markets.

Adventure Attire

For those seeking an adrenaline-pumping experience, pack clothing appropriate for activities such as snorkeling, hiking, and dune bashing. Swimwear, water shoes, and a light jacket are essential for cool nights in the desert.

3

Practical Information

Language and Communication

Arabic is the national language, and its melodious sounds echo through the bustling souks, quiet mosques, and warm hospitality of Oman.mA branch of eastern Arabic, the Omani dialect is characterized by its soft tone and unique vocabulary, often peppered with interesting colloquialisms.

Learning a few basic phrases like "As-salamu alaykum" (peace be upon you) and "Shukran" (thank you) will not only bring smiles and recognition, but also open the door to authentic cultural experiences.

Omanis are masters of non-verbal communication, able to express much with a raised eyebrow and convey warmth and understanding with a gentle hand gesture. Notice the subtle hints that dance with the spoken words.

Direct gaze may be considered rude, but placing your hand over your heart is a sign of sincerity and respect. Due to Oman's emphasis on education and international relations, English is widely spoken, especially in urban areas.

These bilingual language skills make it easier for tourists to go about their daily lives and interact with locals. Don't be surprised if you are greeted with a friendly "Welcome to Oman! After speaking in perfect English, we had a fun conversation about the country's fascinating history and culture.

Venture beyond the major cities and you'll find a kaleidoscope of local dialects, each adding a unique stroke to the linguistic canvas. From the lilting Shihhi spoken along the coast to the rhythmic Bahrawi of the mountainous hinterland, these regional variations offer a glimpse into Oman's rich heritage.

After all, Oman's strongest language is the world language of hospitality. Omanis take great pride in welcoming visitors with open arms and genuine warmth. Regardless of the words exchanged, a smile, a shared kahwa (Omani coffee), and a laugh can bridge any cultural gap.

Dear tourists, as you explore Oman, always remember to listen, be curious, and be open-minded. The language of Oman is a symphony waiting to be heard, a tapestry waiting to be unraveled, an invitation to connect with a culture as rich and vibrant as the sands of the desert.

Useful Apps

Exploring Oman is a journey filled with stunning landscapes, vibrant culture, and warm hospitality. To enrich your experience and move around the country more easily, here is a guide to some useful apps and websites made specifically for tourists in Oman.

Oman Tourism – Oman Experience

Single Use Experience Oman's official app is a treasure trove of information, with comprehensive guides to tourist attractions, events and cultural experiences. It provides information on attractions, accommodations, and local events, making it an essential tool for planning your itinerary.

Google Maps

When it comes to navigation, Google Maps is your trusted companion. It helps you navigate Oman's complex terrain and guides you to attractions, restaurants, and accommodations. Be sure to download offline maps to stay connected in areas with limited connectivity.

Omantel and Ooredoo Apps

Omantel and Ooredoo, Oman's leading telecommunications providers, have easy-to-use apps to help you manage your mobile services, check your data usage, and top up. These apps are useful for staying connected and ensuring a reliable network while traveling.

Zomato and Talabat

Exploring Oman's culinary scene is a must, and apps like Zomato and Talabat make it easy to find local restaurants, read reviews, and enjoy delicious Omani dishes. You can order food right away. From traditional Omani cuisine to international flavors, these apps have something to suit every taste.

Car Rental Apps

If you want to explore Oman by land, consider using car rental apps like Hertz, Budget, or Local Options. These apps make the booking process easy and give you the flexibility to explore the country at your own pace.

Currency Converter App

Oman's currency is the Omani Rial (OMR), so a currency converter app can be very helpful in understanding prices and making an informed purchase.

XE Currency and Currency Calculator Plus are reliable options for real-time exchange rates.

Nizwa Souq App

For an authentic Omani shopping experience, connect to Oman's vibrant markets with the Nizwa Souq app. It provides information about local souks and helps you find traditional crafts, spices and souvenirs.

Weather App

The climate in Oman is variable, so it is very important to be informed about weather conditions when planning outdoor activities. Apps like AccuWeather and Weather.com provide up-to-date weather forecasts to ensure you're prepared for any climate change.

WhatsApp

WhatsApp is a widely used messaging app in Oman, perfect for keeping in touch with friends and family, as well as local businesses, tour operators, and accommodations .

Oman Air and Salam Air Apps

If you're planning a flight within Oman or to neighboring countries, Oman Air and Salam Air's official apps allow you to book flights, check schedules, and manage your reservations.

Money Matters in Oman

Before you pack your bags and dive into the desert world, let's talk about the essential ingredient of any adventure which is money. This guide will provide you with the knowledge you need to easily navigate Oman's financial landscape.

Currency

The official currency of Oman is the Omani Rial (OMR), which is divided into 1,000 Baisa. Think of this as your own magic lamp. You'll have access to fragrant souks, breathtaking desert excursions, and delicious Omani delicacies.

Exchange Rates

Exchange rates can fluctuate like the desert winds, so keep an eye out for great deals. There are ATMs in major cities and tourist areas where you can easily withdraw cash. However, be aware that banks may charge fees for international transactions.

Therefore, please notify us in advance. For large amounts, money exchange offices offer competitive rates, especially when exchanging money into your home currency.

Cash

While cash is still widely accepted, especially in smaller stores and traditional markets, credit cards are becoming more popular in larger cities and tourist establishments. Visa and Mastercard are widely accepted, while American Express and Discover may be less common.

However, in remote areas and small villages, relying solely on plastic may not be a wise decision. With the right mix of cash and cards, your adventure in Oman will go smoothly.

Tipping

Tipping is not compulsory in Oman, but it is always appreciated to show your appreciation. In restaurants, it is customary to leave a small tip of 5-10% of the bill.

Remember, a sincere smile and a polite "shukran" (thank you) go a long way in expressing your gratitude. Oman's lively souks are a treasure trove of handmade goods, spices and souvenirs.

Start with a price well below the asking price and then gradually increase the price with kindness. Remember that respect is key and a smile and friendly conversation often lead to the best deals.

Tip

Download the mobile banking app from Bank to easily monitor your accounts and convert currencies on the go.

Safety in Oman

let's talk about something important safety! We have provided essential emergency contacts to overcome potential dangers and travel in Oman with peace of mind.

Sunscreen

Oman's sun shines with an intensity that rivals the breath of a dragon. Pack a sunscreen with SPF 30 or higher and reapply regularly, especially during rush hour (10am to 4pm).

Seek shade during the day and prefer loose, breathable clothing that covers your shoulders and knees. Respect the sun's fiery embrace, because a sunburn can be an unwanted souvenir.

Hydration Hero

In dry climates, you use water faster than you can open a faucet. Drink plenty of water throughout the day and have a reusable bottle with you.

Choose fresh fruit juice or coconut water for a refreshing, electrolyte-boosting alternative. Dehydration can be an unwanted desert dance, so make sure your inner oasis is well hydrated.

Respect for Local Customs

Oman is a country full of traditions. Dressing modestly in loose, knee-length clothing is not only practical, but also shows respect for local customs. Public displays of affection are frowned upon, so save passionate hugs for private moments.

Safety First, Always Adventure: The allure of the desert is undeniable, but you need to be prepared to venture into its vast environment. Be sure to let someone know your route and travel with a guide or experienced group.

Traffic rules

Traffic rules vary from country to country. Be familiar with Oman's driving regulations, especially on winding mountain roads and busy urban areas. Please be especially careful and remember. Patience is your desert shield.

Emergency Numbers

For any unexpected twists of fate, remember these essential emergency contacts:

- **Police:** 999
- **Ambulance:** 999
- **Fire Department:** 999
- **Tourist Police:** +968 2456 0737

4

Accommodations in Oman

Luxury Resorts and Hotels

Oman, the jewel of the Arabian Peninsula, captivates with its ancient mysticism, breathtaking landscapes and rich culture. And for the discerning traveler seeking unparalleled luxury, Oman's resorts and hotels are a symphony of luxury and tranquility.

Alila Jabal Akhdar

Imagine waking up to clouds kissing your balcony, eagles flying past your window, and the majestic Hajar Mountains stretching as far as the eye can see. This is the reality of Alila Jabal Akhdar. This 2,000 meter resort is a perfect blend of Omani architecture and contemporary design.

Direction: Al Roose, Jabal Al Akhdar Al Jabal Al Akhdar OM, 621, Oman

Six Senses Zighy Bay

Surrounded by the rugged beauty of the Musandam Peninsula, Six Senses Zighy Bay is an oasis of barefoot luxury. Imagine a private villa with an infinity pool overlooking the turquoise waters of the Indian Ocean, a hammam that tells ancient tales of rejuvenation, and a spa where every treatment is a poem for the senses.

Direction: 23°33'04. 58°39'35.8"N 5 Dibba 800, Oman

The Chedi Muscat

Redefining elegance, The Chedi Muscat is an ode to minimalist Omani chic. Its crisp white walls and geometric lines frame the azure expanse of the Gulf of Oman, creating a canvas of tranquility. Luxury in a mirage infinity pool that blends with the horizon, or experience a rejuvenating hammam ritual that kisses your silky skin.

Direction: 133 18th November St, Muscat, Oman

Al Bustan Palace, A Ritz-Carlton Hotel

Reminiscent of an Arabian Nights fairy tale, this vast palace features sparkling fountains, intricately carved archways, and gardens that reveal the secrets of the Sultans. Soak in a private golden pool, enjoy culinary masterpieces at our award-winning restaurant, and immerse yourself in the timeless charm of Omani hospitality.

Direction: Al Bustan St, Muscat 114, Oman

Shangri-La Barr Al Jissah Resort & Spa

Shangri-La Barr Al Jissah Resort & Spa is a paradise for families seeking adventure and relaxation in equal measure. It's a world in itself. Explore hidden coves and colorful coral reefs, conquer the dunes on horseback, or soak up the golden sun on pristine beaches.

Direction: OM, Al Jissah St, 100, Oman

Unique Desert and Mountain Retreats

For those with an adventurous spirit, Oman offers unique desert and mountain getaways that go beyond mere accommodation and serve as gateways to transformative experiences.

Masarrat Al Jissah Beach Resort

Masarrat Al Jissah Beach Resort seamlessly combines desert tranquility with luxurious comfort. Luxury in a private villa with an infinity pool overlooking the endless dunes, pamper yourself with relaxing spa treatments inspired by desert herbs, and embark on an exciting dune adventure.

Arabian Oryx Camp

For an eco-friendly adventure, Oryx Desert Camp is the place to go. This solar-powered camp provides a sustainable retreat using locally sourced materials and a focus on protecting the delicate desert ecosystem. Learn about desert conservation efforts, hike through hidden oases, and witness the graceful dance of oryx at sunset.

Direction: 9PRC+F87, Bidiya, Al Wāṣil 421, Oman

Anantara Al Jabal Al Akhdar Resort

For adventure seekers, Anantara Al Jabal Al Akhdar Resort is a playground above the clouds. Hike through dramatic canyons, climb rock walls through via ferrata, or mountain bike on exciting trails. After a day of adrenaline-pumping activities, relax in a luxurious cliffside villa with a private pool and breathtaking views.

Direction: No 110, Al Jabal Al Akhdar, Nizwa 621, Oman

Budget-Friendly Accommodations

Beyond luxury resorts and luxurious retreats, there is a hidden treasure trove of affordable accommodation to satisfy your adventurous spirit for an authentic Omani experience.

Traditional Homestay

Enjoy warm Omani hospitality at Homestay. Imagine waking up to the smell of freshly baked bread, sharing a meal with a local family, and learning first-hand about their traditions. Homestays like Misfah Old House in Nizwa, with their sun-drenched adobe walls and rooftop terraces, offer a glimpse into a bygone era at surprisingly affordable prices.

Desert Camps Under the Stars

Swap your luxury hotel for a canvas tent in the heart of Wahiba Sands. Desert camps like Al Madar Desert Camp offer an unforgettable experience under the stars. Imagine a night riding a camel through golden sand dunes, stargazing with a local guide, or telling stories under the Milky Way around a crackling campfire.

Boutique Hostels

For solo travelers and budget-conscious adventurers, Oman's boutique hostels offer vibrant social environments and comfortable beds at affordable prices. Hostels like Safari Hostel in Muscat and Salalah Backpackers boast central locations, friendly staff, and opportunities to connect with like-minded travelers from around the world.

Mountain Camping

Oman's dramatic Hajar Mountains are a playground for outdoor enthusiasts. Pitch a tent among juniper forests, hike hidden wadis, and swim in crystal-clear pools. Campgrounds such as Jebel Haat and Jabal Akhdar in Nizwa offer basic facilities and great views, making them perfect for nature lovers on a budget.

Beach bliss on a budget: With over 3,000 kilometers of coastline, Oman has endless options for beach bliss without breaking the bank.

Affordable hotels like Sur Plaza Hotel and City Hotel Duqm offer comfortable accommodation close to pristine beaches, perfect for swimming, sunbathing, and exploring coastal villages.

Tips in Choosing the Right Accomodations

Do you know your travel type

Adventure seeker: Luxury mountain hikes or desert tours? Get a taste of nomadic life at rustic camps in the Hajar Mountains or Wahiba Sands Eco-friendly lodges like Oryx Desert Camp combine comfort and sustainability.

Family Explorer

Shangri-La's Barr Al Jissah Resort & Spa is a family paradise with a water park, kids' club, and adventure activities. Alila Jabal Akhdar offers mountain hiking and stargazing to strengthen family bonds amidst breathtaking scenery.

Prioritize your Needs

Budget: Oman offers something to suit every budget. Luxury resorts like Chedi Muscat and Al Bustan Palace offer luxury, while hostels and homestays offer budget-friendly appeal.

Location

City dwellers can make good money in Muscat, while nature lovers can find mountain retreats such as Jabal Akhdar and desert camps in Wahiba Sands.

Amenities

How about a pool? Dreaming of a spa? Prioritize the essentials, like a private balcony overlooking the ocean or a calming hammam.

Learn some Arabic phrases

A simple "As-salamu alaykum" (peace be upon you) will go a long way in connecting with the locals.

Step out of your comfort zone

Ride a camel in the desert, try traditional Omani crafts, or take a cooking class to learn the secrets of fragrant spices.

Book wisely Off-season travel

Oman's cool season (October to April) offers comfortable temperatures and low prices.

Find offers and package

Many hotels and travel companies offer attractive discounts, especially during the low season. Please consider alternative accommodation. Homestays and boutique hostels offer unique experiences at a fraction of the cost.

5

Muscat: The Capital City

Muscat, the capital of Oman, is a city rich in history and adorned with modern wonders. This is a place where sun-drenched beaches whisper tales of ancient empires and the turquoise Indian Ocean paints the horizon with endless possibilities.

Here you'll find dazzling mosques, bustling souks, and magnificent forts, all waiting to be explored. Fill your heart with wonder and embark on a journey through Muscat's most enchanting treasures:

Sultan Qaboos Grand Mosque

A gleaming white marble masterpiece, the sacred halls of Sultan Qaboos Grand Mosque, This architectural wonder is not only a place of worship but also a testament to Omani art.

Admire the second largest hand-woven Persian rug in the world, stroll through the tranquil courtyard decorated with intricate mosaics, and soak up the atmosphere of spiritual peace.

Royal Opera House Muscat

Muscat's cultural heart beats within the walls of the Royal Opera House. Inspired by Islamic traditions, this architectural gem is a beacon of artistic expression. Experience first-class opera, ballet and musical performances and be immersed in the magical world of theatre.

Mutrah Corniche and Souq

Immerse yourself in the vibrant energy of Mutrah Souk, a maze of narrow streets filled with treasures. Haggle with friendly shopkeepers for intricately woven carpets, handcrafted silver daggers, and fragrant spices.

Breathe in the intoxicating scent of incense and let a cacophony of interaction and laughter surround you. Then, take a stroll along the picturesque Matra Corniche. The turquoise waters of the harbor lap against the shore, and traditional dhows gently rock in the waves.

Al Jalali and Al Mirani Forts

Climb the ancient watchtowers of Al Jalali and Al Mirani Forts. There, cannons whisper stories of battles won and lost. These imposing fortresses perched on rocky cliffs once protected Muscat's port from invaders.

Explore the labyrinth of passageways, peer into hidden rooms, and discover the lives of the soldiers who once guarded these majestic walls. The panoramic views from the ramparts are even more spectacular, offering breathtaking views of the city and the endless sea beyond.

Bait Al Zubair Museum

Step back in time at the Bait Al Zubair Museum, housed in a grand 19th-century Omani mansion. This fascinating museum showcases Oman's rich cultural heritage through displays of traditional clothing, weapons, jewelry, and artifacts. Learn about the country's maritime history, explore the fascinating world of Oman's folklore, and discover the secrets of a bygone era.

Muscat is a city that will captivate your senses and leave you with memories that will last a lifetime. Pack your bags, go on an adventure and discover Muscat's magic. You never know what treasure you'll find around the next corner.

6

Things to Do in Oman

Oman is one of the safest countries in the world and a great destination for couples, solo travelers and families alike. Below are the best tourist attractions and unique activities in Oman.

Ad Dimaniyat Island

Ad Dimaniyat Island Nature Reserve is a great day trip from Muscat. There are nine islands in total, located about 40 minutes from the capital, and are best explored on a tour. This paradise location has the clearest waters you've ever seen and powder-white sand.

The Dimaniyat Islands are famous not only for their turquoise waters, but above all for their incredibly beautiful marine life. You'll see coral reefs, colorful fish, sea turtles, and if you're lucky, you might even spot whale sharks and dolphins. Visiting the Daymaniyat Islands is undoubtedly one of the best things to do in Oman.

Mutrah Souq

Mutrah Souq is one of the oldest souks in Oman and definitely worth a visit. You can spend several hours here just strolling through the small streets. This is the perfect place to get to know the country for the first time.

As soon as you step inside, you'll notice that all your senses are heightened by the aroma. Colorful little shops, locals vying for attention, and the occasional call to prayer from a nearby mosque.

Sultan Qaboos Grand Mosque

Visiting the Sultan Qaboos Grand Mosque is undoubtedly one of his most popular activities in Oman. The amazing architecture of this beautiful building will make you want to take photos again and again. You won't be able to resist.

Try to visit between 8 and 9 a.m, so you can see it before the tour buses arrive. The dress code is very strict here. Men should wear long pants and avoid sleeveless T-shirts with funny logos. A woman should wear a long dress that covers her ankles and wrists and cover her hair with a scarf.

Bimmah Sinkhole

Bimmah Sinkhole is a popular spot for tourists and locals alike. The sinkhole formed when part of the cave collapsed, creating what we see today. Great pool, perfect for swimming. The area around Bimmah Sinkhole has been developed and consists of a small park with picnic tables and a play area for small children.

Admission is free and there is plenty of free parking at the entrance. Bimmah Sinkhole is a great addition to your Oman road trip. You can stop for a quick rest, take a refreshing swim, or just relax for the whole day and enjoy the perfect Omani weather.

Wadi Shab

There is not a single guidebook that does not recommend a visit to Wadi Shab. This is such a great place. Wadi Shab is 2 hours from Muscat.

To get to the pool, you park your car in the parking lot and take a boat that takes you across the river in about 3 minutes. It is a 45 minute hike to the third pool.

It's a relatively easy hike if you wear the right shoes. The third pool is perfect for swimming as the water is crystal clear and the temperature is perfect. Be sure to bring enough water and food for a fun picnic.

Sur

A stop in SUR is a must on any Oman road trip. The city is historically important and famous for its shipyards, where wooden dhows are still built. If you have time, be sure to visit the dhow factory.

At the museum, you can learn how wooden ships were made in the past. Also be sure to visit the lighthouse where you can take beautiful photos and enjoy views of the Gulf of Oman.

Ras Al Jinz Turtle Reserve

Enjoy this unique experience and visit the nesting sites of green sea turtles at Ras Al Jinz Turtle Sanctuary. To see sea turtles, you must book a tour starting at sunrise and sunset. Exact tour times vary depending on the time of year.

Wadi Bani Khalid

There's nothing better when visiting Oman than spending a fun-filled day in the lush wadis. If you're short on time, you can also add Wadi Bani Khalid to your route to Wahiba Sands.

Be sure to allow at least an hour to explore this idyllic location. It is easily accessible and the pool is large, making it perfect for swimming.

Wahiba Sands

One of the most unique things you can do when visiting Oman is, of course, spending a night in the desert. Wahiba Sands is the ideal site for this. Despite the fact that many hotels are situated in isolated desert areas, there's no reason to fear.

Most are completely safe and have everything you need, so you don't have to compromise on comfort. You will need a four-wheel drive vehicle to go to the desert. However, if you do not have a driver, you can ask your hotel to arrange for one to take you to the agreed location.

Nizwa Fort

Surrounded by mountains, this beautiful city is home to Nizwa Fort, one of Oman's most popular forts. Nizwa Fort is strategically located in the city center and consists of a fort and a castle.

This building overlooks a lush palm oasis and the rest of the city. Part of the castle and its maze of cells and rooms have been converted into exhibition halls, and the door opens into a beautiful courtyard.

Al-Jabal Al-Akhdar Mountains

Al Jabal Al Akhhar is also known as the Grand Canyon of the Middle East due to its dramatic landscape. Located at an altitude of 2,000 meters, this area is known for its rosewater, walnuts and pomegranates.

A guided tour will give you great insight into the history of authentic Omani villages scattered throughout the mountains. The hotel will arrange this for you.

Al Hamra

If you're looking for an authentic experience in Oman, don't hesitate to spend a night in Al Hamra Village. This 400-year-old rural village is two hours from Muscat and just 40 minutes from Nizwa.

It is the well-preserved Yemeni-style adobe houses that make a visit to Al Hamra one of Oman's most unique tourist attractions. The village is divided into new and old areas by extensive date plantations.

Strolling through the old town on foot will make you feel as if you have traveled back in time. Don't forget to bring your camera so you can capture the beauty of Al Hamra.

7

Outdoor Adventures in Oman

From sun-drenched sand dunes and rugged mountains to hidden wadis and sparkling coastlines, Oman offers an abundance of outdoor adventures that will get your adrenaline pumping and your soul soaring. Lace up your boots, put on your hat and get ready to soak in the beauty of Oman's natural beauty:

For the Adventurous

Dune Bashing in Wahiba Sands

- Golden sands Imagine racing a four-wheel-drive vehicle over endless waves.
- Let the desert wind blow in your hair as you conquer towering dunes.
- At Wahiba Sands, this exhilarating fantasy becomes a reality.
- Feel the adrenaline rush as you climb giant sand dunes and capture breathtaking sunset photos amidst an endless sea of sand.

Via Ferrata in Jebel Shams

Hike through the special Grand Canyon of Oman. Jebel Shams, the highest mountain in the country, offers a unique experience of traversing steep cliffs, crossing rickety bridges, and rappelling down sheer rock faces.

Enjoy a unique via ferrata experience. Breathtaking scenery and exhilarating challenges will leave you breathless in the best possible way.

Canyoneering in Wadi Ghul

- Immerse yourself in the heart of Oman's dramatic landscape with the Wadi Ghul Canyoning Adventure.
- Hike through narrow gorges, swim in turquoise pools beneath towering cliffs, and rappel down waterfalls while surrounded by the awe-inspiring majesty of Oman's mountains.

For Nature Lovers

Wadi Trekking

- Oman's wadis are lush oases tucked into rugged mountains and a paradise for nature lovers.
- Hike through palm-lined canyons, swim in crystal-clear pools, and picnic in the shadow of towering cliffs. Explore Wadi Bani Khalid, Wadi Shab, or Wadi Darbat.

Whale Watching Off Musandam

- Embark on a boat trip from Musandam and experience the gentle giants of the sea up close.
- See majestic pods of humpback whales crashing through the waves, playful dolphins dancing alongside your boat, and sea turtles gliding

gracefully through the crystal clear waters.

Stargazing in the Desert

- Escape the light pollution and soak in the celestial majesty of the Oman desert.
- Lie under a blanket of stars millions of light-years away and marvel at the Milky Way in pitch black darkness
- The vastness and serenity of the desert sky will leave you humble and awe-struck.

For Water Lovers

Scuba Diving in Musandam Fjords

- Immerse yourself in the underwater wonderland of Musandam Fjord a hidden gem filled with vibrant coral reefs, colorful fish and fascinating marine life.
- Explore shipwrecks, swim through underwater canyons, and witness the graceful dances of stingrays and sharks.

Kayaking in Qurum Beach

- Paddle the turquoise waters of Qurum Beach, a tranquil cove perfect for kayaking adventures.
- Glide in front of fishing boats, spot playful dolphins, and enjoy breath-taking views of Muscat's coastline.

Whether you're looking for an adrenaline-pumping thrill, a quiet escape into nature, or a water adventure, Oman has something to offer every outdoor enthusiast.

Pack your adventurous spirit, grab your swimsuits and hiking boots, and get ready to experience the wild beauty of this enchanting Arabian paradise.

Shopping in Oman

Nestled in the golden sands of the Arabian Peninsula, Oman is a treasure trove waiting to be discovered. While Oman is undoubtedly appealing for its stunning landscapes and rich cultural heritage, it is also a hidden gem for shopaholics.

Mutrah Souq

Immerse yourself in the bustling heart of Muscat at Mutrah Souq, a maze of narrow streets filled with color and scent. Haggle for intricately woven Omani silver jewelry, get lost in the maze of alleyways, and marvel at towering mountains of spices that fill the air with their pungent aromas.

Nizwa Sou

Travel back in time at Nizwa Souk, his 17th century market where time seems to have stopped. Stroll through the labyrinth of stalls filled with handmade pottery, traditional Omani daggers (khanjar), and colorful carpets woven with stories from the past.

Sur Souq

Immerse yourself in the heart of Oman's maritime history at Sur Souq. Stroll through stalls filled with sparkling pearls from the depths of the Arabian Sea, intricately carved wooden dhows, and fragrant incense whose smoky scent recalls ancient trade routes.

Oman Avenues Mall

Enjoy shopping at Oman Avenues Mall, home to international brands and designer boutiques. From high-end fashion and sparkling jewelry to gourmet dining and entertainment options, you can't go wrong with this mall.

Muscat Grand Mall

Immerse yourself in the spaciousness of Muscat Grand Mall, a shopper's paradise with over 350 stores. Fashion stores, home goods stores and electronics stores all under one roof.

Salalah Gardens Mall

Escape the Omani sun and enjoy the cool comfort of Salalah Gardens Mall. Browse a selection of local and international brands, dine at international restaurants and catch a movie at a state-of-the-art movie theater.

Discover Hidden Gems

Art galleries

Oman is an emerging center for contemporary art. Find unique works by local and international artists showcasing their talents at galleries such as Bait Muzna in Muscat and Oman Fine Arts Society in Salalah.

Carpets and Textiles

Immerse yourself in the vibrant world of Omani carpets and textiles. Visit workshops in Nizwa and Sur to see the intricate weaving process and purchase unique carpets and hand-woven scarves.

Spices and incense

Enjoy the enchanting aromas of Oman's spice market. Get scented blends for your kitchen or choose from a variety of incense sticks whose smoky scent fills your home with the essence of the Arabian Peninsula.

Experience the Shopping Experience

Shopping in Oman is about more than just acquiring treasures. Remember that Omanis are known for their hospitality. So, don't hesitate to strike up a conversation and learn more about the rich cultural heritage behind each handmade item.

8

Omani Culture and Traditions

Traditional Omani Cuisine

One of the wonders of Oman's unique culture is its exceptionally delicious traditional cuisine. From dates and coffee to rice and grilled meat, here are the best Omani dishes that every visitor must try when visiting the country.

Majboos

Majboos, also known as kabsa or maqboos, is a traditional mixed rice dish that originated in Saudi Arabia. It is famous in the Arab world, especially in the Gulf countries, including Oman.

This dish consists of rice, usually basmati, vegetables, meat or poultry, and a mixture of spices. It may also be served with yogurt or a green salad, traditional bread, and tomato sauce.

Shuwa

Shuwa means grilled meat in Arabic. It is a popular dish in Oman and is often prepared on special occasions such as Eid.

In fact, Omanis usually prepare meat on the first day of Eid and eat it on the second or third day. Shuwa is marinated in Omani spices, wrapped in banana leaves or palm leaves, and baked in an underground sand oven for one to two days.

Omani Bread

Omani bread comes in many varieties. The other one is crunchy and thin, about the size of a small round plate. Most Omanis bake bread at home, but there are also bakeries. Bread is often served with meals at restaurants.

Date

The most common plantations in Oman are palm trees. They produce delicious dates. These dates, which vary in size, color and softness, are one of the essential meals served to all guests as part of great Omani hospitality.

Omanis sometimes mix dried dates with sesame paste, sesame seeds, or ground coconut. We also use them to make different types of desserts and Omani sweets.

Kahwa

Kahwa means coffee in Arabic. It is famous not only for its taste and texture, but also for its cultivation, drying, and cooking methods.

Like dates, they are an essential part of Omani hospitality and are also served with Omani halwa (dessert). Most Omanis drink kaffa several times a day.

Meshkak

Meshkak, also known as kebab, is marinated beef, mutton, or chicken grilled on stickers. It is usually marinated with various spices, especially curry, and served with Omani bread. This is also a special dish in Oman and is made all over the country, especially during celebrations.

Halwa

Halwa means dessert in Arabic. However, halwa is also the name of the most famous Omani sweet. It is characterized by its richness, which is thicker than custard. Although halwa is brown in color, no chocolate is used in its preparation.

Omani halwa consists of sugar, honey, rose water, eggs, several Omani spices, and nuts. It is usually served with kapha and dates. Omanis serve it on a large plate with a few spoons so that guests and visitors can share the delicacy.

Mashuai

Mashuai is a delicious Omani fish dish. Grilled kingfish topped with a special spicy lemon sauce. Using traditional Omani spices, this dish is uniquely delicious and is not to be missed when visiting the country.

Best Restaraunts in Oman

Whether you're into traditional Omani cuisine, Indian cuisine or international cuisine, Oman's capital is full of delicious restaurants. This list will help you choose between a variety of restaurants, from the best seafood dishes to the best traditional Omani restaurants.

Bait Al Luban

Across from the fish market in the Muttrah Souk district is Bait Al Luban, a classic Omani restaurant in Muscat. It is set in a traditional guesthouse and offers beautiful sea views.

Visitors are greeted with complimentary scented water to get a taste of Omani culture. It serves traditional Omani dishes, including the famous shuwa, a marinated meat roasted in an underground oven for over six hours.

Address: harat a'shamal street مسقط OM MUTTRAH CORNICHE OM، 130, Oman

Ubhar Restaurant

is a modern take on traditional Omani cuisine, serving everything from halwa pastries to slow-roasted camel shuwa. Located near the famous Royal Opera House Muscat, it's the perfect place to combine dinner and a show.

The furniture is of high quality, with a choice of both traditional Omani-style seating and Western chairs. Don't miss the chance to try frankincense ice cream, Oman's true desert variety.

Address: Al Kharjiyah St مسقط OM, 100, Oman

Asado South American Steakhouse

If you're craving a hearty steak after exploring Oman, there's no better option than Asado South American Steakhouse at the Sheraton Oman. They offer a variety of cuts of meat, including sirloin, ribeye steak, Wagyu beef, and tomahawk.

The restaurant features a stylish design and also serves other imaginative dishes such as Brazilian mango mouse cake and ceviche that is sure to put a smile on your face.

Address: 40 Way, Muscat 112, Oman

Mumtaz Mahal

One of Muscat's most famous restaurants, Mumtaz Mahal is the home of authentic Indian cuisine. There are several beautifully decorated dining rooms as well as a wonderful seating area with terrace views.

It has been awarded Oman's Best Indian Restaurant 10 times for its authentic cuisine of classic Mughlai and Punjabi cuisine. These include tandoori prawns, chicken tikka, mutton curry and more.

Address: Box 1142 Qurum OM, 114, Oman

Mani's Cafe Oman

Located in the cosmopolitan Al Mouj district, Mani's Cafe Oman is a popular restaurant for expats and locals alike. Popular items on the breakfast menu include spicy eggs with mozzarella and chili.

The eggs Benedict with side salad was cooked to perfection, as was the sweet French toast with maple syrup and freshly brewed coffee.

Address: Marsa 2, Muscat 130, Oman

Tuscany Restaurant, Muscat

As Grand Hyatt's signature restaurant, Tuscany brings a high level of charm and flavor to the capital. Traditional design and artwork give guests the feeling of entering a Roman temple.

The outdoor patio offers stunning bay views and a romantic atmosphere perfect for a date night. Popular dishes include pizzas, risotto, and pasta. A carefully selected wine selection is also available to accompany the classic Italian cuisine.

Address: Grand Hyatt Muscat, Shatti Al Qurm, Muscat, Oman Muscat OM, 133, Oman

China Mood Restaurant, Muscat Oman

Fine dining restaurant China Mood is located at Al Bustan Palace, a Ritz-Carlton hotel.

This fine-dining restaurant serves one of the best Chinese dishes in Muscat, pairing dishes such as fried lamb chops, duck spring rolls, foie gras dumplings, and Peking duck with rich plum sauce and pancakes.

Address: Al Bustan Palace Ritz-Carlton Hotel, Muttrah Muscat OM, 114, Oman

D'Arcy's Kitchen

Located in Muscat's Qurum Beach area, D'Arcy's Kitchen Kitchen is a popular hangout for expats and locals alike, offering a variety of breakfast and lunch dishes.

The atmosphere at D'Arcy's has a unique home-like feel, and the restaurant is known for its all-day breakfast menu, including Country English Breakfast and Traditional American Breakfast. They also offer delicious sandwiches, burritos, and brioche French toast.

Festivals and Celebrations in Oman

A festive atmosphere fills the air as Oman's golden sands sparkle under the Arabian sun. Festivals in Oman are more than just events. They are a living expression of the country's rich cultural heritage, inviting tourists into a world where tradition lives in a symphony of colour, rhythm and warmth.

Muscat Festival

Held annually (January-February), Muscat Festival is a kaleidoscope of cultural, artistic, and gastronomic performances. The city turns into a living tapestry, reverberating with traditional Omani music, folklore, and a mouth-watering selection of local cuisine.

From vibrant parades to mesmerizing fireworks displays, Muscat Festival is a feast for the senses that introduces tourists to Oman's heritage.

Renaissance Day

On 23 July, Oman celebrates Renaissance Day, marking the accession of His Majesty Sultan Qaboos bin Said to the throne. Festivals are held across the country that combine traditional elements with modern flair. Streets are decorated with national flags and locals take part in parades, concerts and cultural events to mark Oman's path of progress and unity.

Eid al-Fitr

Eid al-Fitr, the festival marking the end of Ramadan, is a joyous occasion celebrated with enthusiasm and compassion. The spirit of giving is felt as families gather for celebrations, exchange gifts, and participate in charitable activities.

Tourists have the opportunity to witness the communal prayers, colorful processions and great festive atmosphere that surround Oman's cities and towns.

Salalah Tourism Festival

During the kharif (monsoon) season, Salalah hosts the Salalah Tourism Festival. The festival is a unique celebration that combines cultural performances, traditional dance performances, and the natural beauty of the region.

Visitors can immerse themselves in the cultural heritage of Dhofar Special Region, enjoy local cuisine and explore the lush landscape that comes alive during this special time.

National Day

Oman's National Day, 18 November, is a day to celebrate the country's unity and progress. The streets are decorated with national colors and the air is filled with patriotic fervor.

Celebrations include parades, traditional dancing, and a spectacular fireworks display, allowing visitors to experience first-hand Omani pride and unity.

Oman Women's Day

Oman Women's Day, celebrated on October 17, is a special day to recognize the contribution of Omani women to the country's progress. Celebrations will include cultural events, exhibitions and discussions highlighting the achievements and empowerment of women in Oman. Tourists can witness the dynamism of Omani women in various fields.

Camel Racing Festival

Camel racing has a special place in Omani culture, and festivals dedicated to this traditional sport showcase the strength and agility of these amazing creatures . Visitors can witness exciting races, marvel at the skillful handling of camels, and experience the lively atmosphere surrounding these events.

In Oman, festivals are a gateway into the soul of the nation, offering travelers the opportunity to immerse themselves in Oman's warm hospitality, witness centuries of tradition, and celebrate the modern vibrancy of this fascinating country.

9

conclusion

As you draw the final curtain on your exploration through the pages of our Oman travel guide, stop and enjoy a wonderful journey through this jewel of Arabia. Rugged landscapes, age-old traditions and warm hospitality have proven that Oman is more than just a destination, it is a fascinating chapter in your travel story.

From the timeless beauty of Sultan Qaboos Grand Mosque to Muscat's labyrinthine souks, each section of this guide was a key to unlocking Oman's treasures. The whispers of the Wahiba sand dunes, the turquoise waters of Musandam's fjords and the aromatic flavors of Omani cuisine will be treasured memories etched into your travel diary.

May the insights and recommendations gathered here serve as a compass for your future desert adventures, coastal explorations, and cultural experiences. May Oman continue to be your guide, whether you marvel at historic forts, stroll through ancient markets or marvel at the ethereal beauty of the desert night sky.

May your memories of Oman continue to awaken your wanderlust. Until we meet again, your journey will be as enchanting as the one you find in this Arabian gem, whether among rugged mountains, along a pristine coastline or inside a vibrant souk, I hope it becomes something.

Safe Travels!

Printed in Great Britain
by Amazon

46738458R00050